LEADERSHIP

Magnolia-Anaheim Day Center
10425 Magnolia Ave.
Anaheim, CA 92804

Leadership is a type of interpersonal skill—a skill that helps you to work well with others.

THE SCHOOL-TO-WORK LIBRARY

LEADERSHIP

Julie Parker

GLOBE FEARON EDUCATIONAL PUBLISHER
A Division of Simon & Schuster
Upper Saddle River, New Jersey

To a courageous leader, Bishop C. Dale White.

Published in 1996 by The Rosen Publishing Group, Inc.
29 East 21st Street, New York, NY 10010

First Edition

Printed in the United States of America

ISBN 0-835-91788-6

Contents

Introduction

DO YOU HAVE A POSITIVE EFFECT ON OTHERS?
Do you like to motivate people toward a common goal? Are you able to work with others and get things done? Today's world needs strong, creative, and committed leaders. As schools, jobs, and much of society become more competitive, your ability as a leader can set you apart. This book is designed to help you develop your leadership talent to use at school, at work, and in your career.

But it is important to remember that there can be no leaders without followers. Although many books and articles are written about leadership, no one seems to pay much attention to "followership." You can be the greatest leader in the world, but if you are trying to get people involved in a cause that no one cares about, you're only a lonely crusader.

Also, the people who lead in some situations naturally follow in others. For example, you may lead your teammates as the captain of the baseball team and follow the conductor as a member of the school

The ability to motivate others is one of the building blocks of leadership.

orchestra. Leading is not "better" than following; they are two different skills that go hand-in-hand. Both are skills you can learn.

Historically, some leaders were born into families that already held leadership positions. They simply assumed titles, such as "king" or "queen", that were handed down to them.

Although money and social status still make it easier for some people to reach positions of power, today's leaders come from all levels of society. For example, President Bill Clinton was the middle-class son of a hard-working single mother.

Nonetheless, it is more difficult for some people to become leaders than others. People often have a narrow view of what a great leader should look like. Unfortunately, it seems that many people picture a strong leader as a good-looking, tall, middle-aged, physically fit white man. Even without realizing it, they may discriminate against someone who does not match their image. Since few of us fit this description, you may find that people do not expect you to be a leader because of your race, gender, age, weight, or height. That does not mean that you can't become an effective leader, but it does mean that you may have to work harder for people to notice and appreciate what you are able to do. Fortunately, the public's view of leadership seems to be changing, though slowly. There are more women, people of color, and people with disabilities in leadership positions than there have been in the past.

As you read this book, you will discover how you can develop yourself as a leader. You will also learn about mistakes that leaders often make, and how you can avoid them. Your ability as a leader—and your appreciation of followers—can be your ticket to a successful future.

Customers are more responsive to employees who are neat, articulate, and enthusiastic, showing clear evidence of leadership.

Follow the Leader

AS A LEADER, YOU NEED TO PROJECT YOURSELF well by acting with courtesy and confidence. This lets people see that you are respectful, have goals, and are working to accomplish them. Simple aspects of everyday behavior, like the way you dress and stand and speak, send a message about who you are. People form impressions right away and decide, sometimes without knowing it, whether or not they want to listen to you.

Sending the Right Signals

Be aware of the silent signals you send. Suppose you have just started a job at a local clothing store. If you walk into work with your hair uncombed, wearing wrinkled clothes, and slouching against the clothing racks, you will appear uninterested in your work even if you do care about it. On the other hand, if you dress appropriately for that store, know about the merchandise, and act helpful but not too pushy, customers will come to you. They will seek your help, and eventually the management will notice you. Your personal presence and appearance will mark you as a leader.

Another important part of leading people is communicating clearly and effectively. Be sure to listen attentively to what people say. Respond appropriately, and let them know that you understand their concerns. Speak as well as you can, and choose your words carefully, especially when speaking about something you feel strongly about. When you are talking one-on-one, be polite, honest, and direct. If you are addressing a group, stand tall and speak clearly.

Many people feel uncomfortable talking in front of a group of people. If you do, you may want to take a speech class or work with a theater coach to improve your public speaking. Sometimes just practicing in front of a mirror helps. Try to feel, or at least seem, at ease when you talk to a group.

Getting People's Attention

Let's say you are organizing a volunteer Adopt-a-Grandparent program between your high school and a nearby nursing home. What do you think will happen if you gather your volunteers for a meeting, stand in the front of the room, act embarrassed, and say, "... Um ... excuse me ... could you listen to me? ... Hello ..."? People will barely notice you. On

A speech or drama class can be a way to gain experience and confidence speaking in front of groups of people.

the other hand, when you get up with a sense of purpose, stand straight, and call for people's attention, you send a message about your ability as a leader. By saying in a strong voice, "Listen up, everyone, please. I want to thank all of you for coming. I have important information to share," people will tune in to what you are saying.

Once you have their attention, you need to make good use of it. Most people today have many demands on their time; they are giving you some of their time, so make the most of it. Be prepared. Do your research, preparation, and planning before you address a group. Know in advance what you want to say to others, while staying flexible about using their suggestions.

Follow through on what you say you will do. It is tempting for leaders to agree to take on a project and then abandon or forget about their promises. But people remember if you are reliable. Think twice before you say you will do something. And once you have agreed to it—do it!

Setting Goals

Remember that people have agreed to work with you toward a goal. Have a plan, and move toward accomplishments. Set priorities about what is most important.

Suppose you work as a lifeguard at the town pool. You've been there for three summers and have really impressed the supervisor. This year, you have been asked to be the head lifeguard. One of your primary responsibilities is to teach the new life-guards about their jobs. You will want to teach them about their role and about the rules of the pool before you talk about the schedule for lunch breaks. That is because safety is the top priority.

With a clear goal, you and your co-workers can create a safe, enjoyable environment. While you need to have clear goals, you should also be reason-able in what you expect. For example, if you gave the other lifeguards a list of chores that were not part of their jobs—such as cleaning the bathrooms and emptying the garbage—they would resent you. The lifeguards would not go out of their way to help you with new chores that come up because they would already feel overloaded. You can help avoid others' burnout, and your own. Find a balance; get people to commit themselves to projects, but don't ask them to do so much that they feel burdened.

You will also lead well when you adapt to situations easily and make necessary changes. Take the opportunity to handle a situation before it becomes a bigger problem. Try to get in the habit of saying, "We can work it out," or "That shouldn't be too much of a problem," when someone approaches you with a difficulty that can be resolved. If you do this, others will find that they can turn to you with concerns.

If you respond to someone's problem by saying, "You did what? How could you be so stupid?", people will not feel comfortable coming to you with issues that need to be addressed. The situation will probably get worse. If you are the leader, the responsibility of getting things worked out falls heavily on you. And when all goes well, you will be credited for your part in guiding the effort.

Two Types of Power
As you develop your leadership skills, realize that

Keep a positive attitude when approaching others about their problems or concerns.

there are two kinds of power that leaders can use to reach their goals. Formal power comes with a position. Examples of people with formal power include the boss in an office, the manager of a store, the president of a club, or the teacher in a classroom. Informal power comes from popularity. If you are liked and respected, people are much more likely to listen to you and want to work with you. Part of being a good leader is recognizing which type of power is available to you and learning how to use it.

At the same time, remember that leading is a privilege. A leader has the opportunity to inspire others to work together. If people trust you to be their leader, you need to be worthy of their trust.

This means that you must act morally, or in ways that do not hurt others. You must make ethical decisions that are honest and considerate. Cheating or tricking or stealing has led to the downfall of many people who were considered great leaders but are now remembered as traitors. Never forget that with privilege comes responsibility.

Questions to Ask Yourself

Communicating well with others and setting goals are important parts of leadership. 1) Do you pay attention to your appearance and behavior? 2) Do you speak clearly and effectively? Are you comfortable speaking before a group of people? 3) Do you work toward your goals single-mindedly?

Lead the Follower

As you develop and practice your leadership skills, remember that the nature of leadership is changing. The most successful companies and organizations no longer think that leaders should simply direct others. Leadership is about working *with* people, not over them. As a leader, you are expected to recognize good ideas and put them into action. You need to create an environment in which people know that their ideas are valuable.

To do this, you first must gain others' respect. And the only way to be respected is to respect others. The best way to show respect is to listen. When someone is talking to you, make eye contact. Do not interrupt. Comment on what is said, or ask a question if you need more information. Even if you totally disagree with what is said, mention at least one thing that you found helpful before you add your own point of view.

Learn people's names. Concentrate when you are introduced to someone and try hard to remember

Make eye contact and try to remember people's names in social situations.

what they are called. If necessary, use the trick of associating something about the person with his or her name. For example, suppose you are running a meeting of the Spanish Club and a new person shows up. Before the meeting starts, go over to introduce yourself and welcome her. Her name is Pam, and you associate that with the pale color of her sweater by thinking to yourself, "Pam Pale." Later when she offers a suggestion and you say, "Thanks, Pam," you will have done a lot to gain her trust. Of course, you have to use that first meeting to really learn her name, so you will still know it when she wears something else.

When you let someone know that you appreciate

what they have said or done, everyone wins. Some leaders are slow to tell others what a good job they did, because they think it makes it look as if they themselves have done less. The opposite is true. When you thank people for their help, they feel rewarded and recognized for their time and effort. As a result, they are more likely to help in the future. It also adds to your image as a leader, because you are behaving with confidence. You seem inwardly secure and outwardly gracious.

Just as you value others' contributions of time and energy, value their input. People who are joining with you on a project, like running for a school office or creating a student volunteer club, are there because they care about it too. What do they hope will happen? How can your group pursue useful ideas? Once you've heard people's suggestions for improvements and possibilities, follow up on them. Decide what is worth developing and do it.

Delegating Tasks

If you are leading a large project or working with a lot of people, be sure to delegate or share responsibilities. Ask a specific person to do a certain task and let her or him know exactly what is involved. Then check back later to see if there are any problems. If you try to do everything yourself, you weaken your group and exhaust yourself. By dividing the

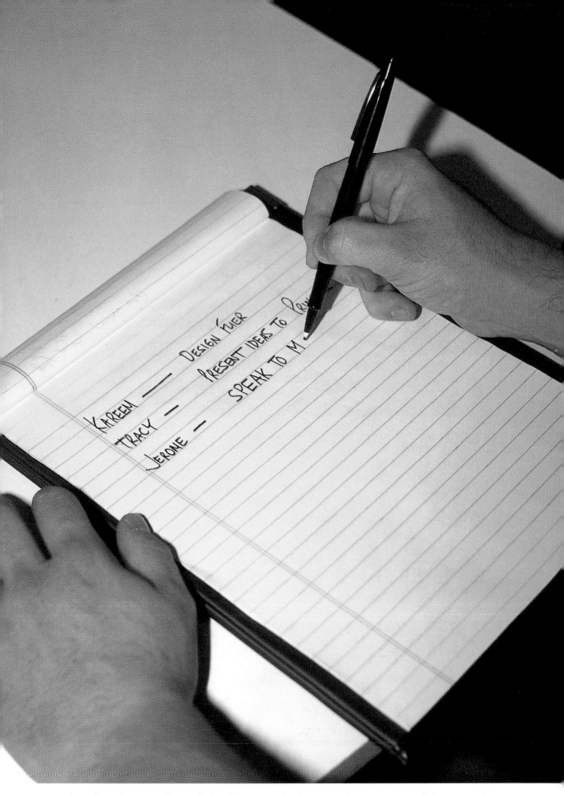

Make a list of your tasks and check to see whether any of your responsibilities can be given to others.

When campaigning for a position in student government, you might enlist the help of friends to help you win votes.

workload, you give others a significant role that increases their commitment and confidence.

As an effective leader, you need to keep people involved. When people show up at a meeting, find a way to make the most of their talents; people power is too valuable to waste.

Never position people against each other. Let's say you're running for president of the student body, and you hold a meeting for people who want to work on your campaign. It would not be smart to divide your volunteers into two groups, asking each to come up with a campaign slogan so you can choose one. The group whose slogan you didn't choose might feel that you have unfairly rejected their idea and wasted their time.

Even though it takes energy and effort, the process of reaching a goal is as important as getting there. Have everyone work on creating a slogan together. Call it a creative brainstorming session. Bring markers or crayons so people can draw images to go with their words. If it's a small group and you can afford it, bring along some snacks. Try to make the session fun. Make sure you know everyone, and then introduce people. Most people enjoy making friends, and this is a great way to do it.

Remember that you lead best by example. Rather than talking on and on about the need for students to serve lunch at a local soup kitchen, you are far more convincing when you just do it yourself. Your actions show the importance that you place on a certain task, and that speaks louder than words. Your commitment will inspire others.

The art of good leadership is finding a balance. If you ask people to do too much, they may burn out, and you will lose them. But if you ask them to do too little, they may withdraw, feeling that their participation really isn't necessary. Pour your energy into reaching your goal, and you will motivate others to work with you.

Experts have divided leadership skills into three broad categories:

- **Diagnostic skills.** These skills include critical and creative thinking and problem-solving.
- **Perceptual skills.** These skills involve communicating well through good verbal and listening skills.
- **Behavioral skills.** These skills include teamwork, team building, negotiation, delegation, motivation, coaching, and counseling.

As you can see, leadership involves many different skills. Some skills may come naturally to you; you may need to work harder on others. For example, you may be great at listening to people's problems and giving advice, but uncomfortable negotiating with others. The better you can use your strengths and work on your weaknesses, the more effective you'll be as a leader.

Questions to Ask Yourself

Effective leaders strike a balance between motivating others and helping them to motivate themselves. 1) Do you work well with people? 2) Do you notice and express appreciation when someone does a good job? When you are in charge, do you delegate tasks to others? 3) What are the skills of leadership?

Moving Ahead at School

SCHOOL IS A GREAT PLACE TO LEARN
leadership. As you study and have fun with your friends, you also have the chance to explore what you might want to do later in your life. You don't need to rush to figure out what your career is going to be; simply by taking classes and trying activities you will discover what you are good at and what you enjoy. This will naturally bring you to the areas where you can learn to be a capable leader.

School as a Leader's Laboratory

In a school you have a community of people gathered to accomplish goals—learning, teaching, or working. Because of this, school is like a leader's laboratory. By watching and becoming involved, you can find out what makes a strong leader.

One way to begin is by observing. Look at the adults in positions of authority: the principal, the vice principal, the teachers, the guidance counselors. Who is the most respected? Take a day as you go

Teachers who keep students engaged and interested are effective leaders.

through your classes to note effective leadership styles. Why does one teacher keep a class's attention, while another has the same students daydreaming, and a third struggles to keep them from being loud and rowdy?

You will probably discover some similarities among the teachers who are the best leaders. First, they are committed to their subjects. They enjoy whatever subject they are teaching. Second, they respect students and treat them intelligently. This means not only talking to them with courtesy, but listening to them with consideration. Third, they are prepared. They don't just come into class and ramble on and on. They have a thought-out lesson plan.

Depending on the individual teacher's personality, you may notice other factors that contribute to impressive leadership. A teacher may be funny and use humor to interest students. Maybe a teacher has a way of talking or illustrating points that makes the material seem interesting. Perhaps the most powerful way for a teacher, or any leader, to get someone's attention is to address the listener's concerns.

Listening and Learning

Naomi wants to run for president of the sophomore class. She is considering a career in law or politics.

To run for office, she first needs to gather fifty signatures. Once she is on the ballot, she must give a speech in a class assembly. Naomi gets to work.

First, she types up a signature sheet and goes around school asking people to sign. Most people sign it because they know her and think she's nice enough. That part is easy. But once she realizes that she's going to have to speak to all the sophomores in an assembly, Naomi starts to panic. She has no idea what she will say.

As the day of the assembly gets closer, Naomi has a hard time sleeping. One night she tosses and turns and eventually comes up with an idea. She decides that she will propose a sophomore dance, like the junior and senior proms. The next day in the cafeteria she tests her idea on her friends Rhonda, Jenny, and Deborah.

"Hey, you guys," Naomi begins casually, while dipping her french fry in ketchup, "what do you think of a sophomore dance for our class? Why should only the juniors and seniors have the fun?"

"What do you mean?" answers Rhonda. "Their fun is my fun. I'm going to the senior prom."

"Oh, yeah, who's asking you?" chimes in Deborah.

"Some lucky guy, yet to be determined . . ." Rhonda tells her, and they all laugh.

"Who wants to do all the work for a dance?" asks

School can provide opportunities to lead others in school activities or projects.

Jenny. "Besides, where would you have it? In this dumpy cafeteria?"

"At least that would use the cafeteria for *something*," says Deborah.

Naomi is puzzled. "What do you mean?"

"Haven't you heard?" Deborah says. "They're cutting the school breakfast program. They say it doesn't matter that much to the students, and it's too expensive. I'm really bummed about it. I never eat breakfast at home. When I leave the house in the morning my family is still asleep."

As the talk continues, Naomi discovers that this is an issue already on people's minds. Although she usually eats breakfast at home, Naomi comes to

29

school early the next morning to see how the program works. She notices that, while the cafeteria never looks full, a lot of students drift in, get something to eat, and then leave. Naomi asks some of these students if they know that the breakfast program might be cut. Many of them are surprised and angry.

Soon, it becomes clear to Naomi that this is an issue for her campaign. She starts looking into what steps she could take as class president to work on keeping the breakfast program, even if it offered only a cold breakfast. Suddenly she discovers that she has more than enough to say for her assembly speech. And she is sure that she will have the attention of the other students—the voters—in her class.

Naomi is practicing an important leadership skill that every politician knows: In order to lead, you first must follow. When she is in touch with what people want, need, or care about, they will be interested in what she has to say.

She is also realizing the difference between being popular and being a leader. Naomi was able to get fifty people to sign her petition because she is fairly popular. Being liked already gives her some informal power. But the difference between leading and being popular is having goals. Naomi wants to get elected, then she wants to save the breakfast program. With clear goals she becomes a leader—which is different from simply being a popular person.

Using Your Ambition

If you are reading this book, you want to be a leader. You have ambition. This drive to succeed pushes you to reach your goals. How do you use your ambition in school? Do you study hard so you can get into a good college? Do you devote your time after school to the school newspaper so you can become editor-in-chief? Do you practice running and lifting weights so you can do well on a sports team? These are positive uses of ambition, as long as you don't let your intentions take over your sense of reason or fairness. Doing that could harm others or yourself.

Paul is a junior in high school who runs on the cross-country track team. He loves to compete. Even though he just started running track this year, he is already the fastest on the team. Paul's impressive race times have helped the team to get to the state championship track meet. The other team members are all excited and know that Paul is their star runner. He was elected captain of the team, even though he isn't a senior. Paul enjoys the status of being the leader.

One day after practice, Paul sees Michael hanging out by the fence on the edge of the track. Paul recognizes him as someone who graduated from the high school last year. Michael calls Paul over.

"Hey, you, what's your name?" Michael asks.

"Paul. Why?"

"Listen, Paul, I hear you're pretty good," Michael continues.

"How do you know?"

"Some of the guys were telling me about you."

"Really? Who?" Paul asks, suddenly interested.

"Oh, you know, David," answers Michael.

Paul was about to ask him which David, since there were three on the team, but Michael went on.

"Listen, I hear you're on your way to a big race. I came here to help you win."

"Help us win? How?" asks Paul.

"Come here," Michael says, opening his hand to reveal a small white pill. "This. Only twenty dollars a hit. Pop this before the meet and your team will be the state champs. Your time will leave the others in the dust. No one will ever know. Don't you want to win? The state championship can be yours. Guaranteed."

Paul is stunned. "What do I need that for?" he says, walking away. "I'm doing fine."

Michael follows him. "Sure you are, against the little teams around here. But now you're headed for real competition. Do you want to let your team down? Everyone is counting on you. The guys will be real disappointed if you don't come through."

Paul starts thinking about all the pressure he has been feeling. His friends on the team have been talking about nothing but the meet, and Paul feels it's all up to him. Having a pill as a back-up plan doesn't seem like a bad idea. He's already come close to breaking some state records; this could put him over the top. Then he probably would have no problem getting a track scholarship to college. Paul isn't sure what to do. And Michael won't leave him alone.

Paul needs to be careful that his desire to lead doesn't cause him to fail. The risks of taking drugs are many. A drug could do serious harm to his body, including decreasing—or even destroying—his running ability. It might affect his mind or his judgment or speech. There is a strong possibility that he would be caught taking the drug, which would disqualify him and really let his teammates down. He might even risk being expelled. The choice not to take drugs seems obvious.

However, powerful ambition can lead people to make foolish decisions. Sometimes people want so badly to win or succeed that they will do anything, even if it means hurting themselves or others. You

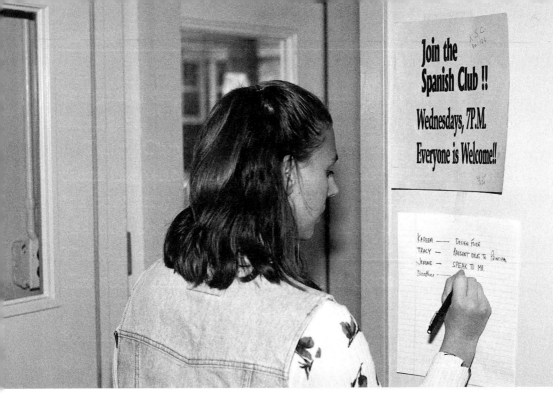

Joining a club or team is the first step to achieving a leadership position.

need to keep your ambition focused on positive goals and avoid destructive ways of accomplishing them. Your school gives you many chances to do this.

Using Opportunities

Perhaps the most important factor of leadership is simply taking advantage of the chance to lead. The clubs, teams, classes, and events that take place at school need leadership if anything positive is to happen. Since the student population is always changing, new leaders are always in demand. Don't be afraid to try to take a leadership position such as president, editor, or team captain.

Sharon came back to school after a trip during the summer with her aunt. As a special birthday present, Sharon's Aunt Eleanor took her on a three-week tour of Europe. Sharon returned home thrilled about all that she had seen and eager to travel more. She thinks that she'd like a career that involves travel, maybe as a flight attendant or a tour guide, or even in international relations.

As soon as the new school year begins, Sharon becomes involved in the foreign exchange club that hosts students from abroad. Late in the spring the club has elections for the next year. Mr. Clements, the exchange club adviser, talks to Sharon on her way out of a meeting.

"Hey, Sharon," he begins, "you've been an important part of the club this year . . . Have you thought about running for an office?"

Sharon has thought about it because she likes the club so much and never misses a meeting, but she isn't sure if she can do it.

"Well, doesn't it take a lot of time?" Sharon asks.

"You give a lot of time anyway," Mr. Clements points out. "And you seem to have good ideas for the group."

"Yeah, it's a great club, but I'm just not sure if I'm the type to be an officer . . ." Sharon continues.

Mr. Clements seems surprised. "Why not?"

"I don't know... I just haven't held an office before," Sharon shrugs.

"Well, I think you've got the dedication and ideas we need. Just tell me you'll give it some thought, okay?" asks Mr. Clements.

"Okay, sure," Sharon says, and leaves. Secretly, she feels honored that Mr. Clements thinks she would be a good leader. She hadn't even realized that he noticed how much she enjoys the club. But for reasons she can't explain, Sharon feels a little scared at the idea of being an officer.

Sharon has many of the qualities that it takes to be a leader—energy, commitment, enthusiasm, dedication, ideas—but she lacks confidence. She just doesn't picture herself in this role, even though the experience would be valuable for careers that interest her, like leading tours. However, other people recognize and appreciate Sharon's commitment and potential. Sharon needs to stop and ask herself why Mr. Clements wants her to try to win a leadership role. Then she might see some of the same characteristics in herself that he sees.

She might also find out what is involved in a leadership role. What are the duties of the president, vice president, secretary, and treasurer? Often, when you break down the responsibilities, the positions seem more manageable. If there is too much for

Use time alone to give serious thought to the special strengths you can bring to a leadership role.

one person to do, the leader can—and should—ask others to do some of the tasks.

But she is also afraid that she will not be elected. What if she loses? Sharon would feel awful, and so she isn't sure that she wants to try. In her mind, it is as if she has already lost.

Sharon needs to realize that she has nothing to lose. She's a club member now, and that's what she would be if she didn't get elected. At least she owes it to herself and Mr. Clements to do what she said she would: give a leadership role some serious consideration. She might end up surprising herself with all she can do. As the saying goes, it's better to have tried and failed than never to have tried at all.

Learning about Yourself

You may surprise yourself, too, as you take on leadership roles in school. Having this experience can be valuable for you personally, academically, and professionally. As an individual, you learn about your strengths, weaknesses, and abilities. As a student, you are contributing to the school community, while figuring out how to balance your own time and make the most of your studies. As you advance toward your career, you will be prepared to be a leader. Future college and job applications will ask about your involvement in extracurricular activities. If you have been a leader, you will be perceived as someone with vision, commitment, and a drive to succeed.

Questions to Ask Yourself

School offers many opportunities for gaining leadership skills. 1) Which of your teachers do you see as a leader? 2) What makes that teacher a leader? 3) What is the difference between popularity and leadership? Which will take you faster toward your goal?

Moving Ahead at Work

IN THE BROADWAY MUSICAL *HOW TO SUCCEED* *in Business Without Really Trying*, a window washer named J. Pierrepont Finch rises to the head of a large company without doing much work. Instead, he gets his foot in the door, looks like he's busy, but really spends his time getting noticed and liked by the company president. Finch is constantly telling and spelling his name so that the people in power will remember him. By the time the final curtain comes down, Finch is the president of the Board of Trustees.

All of this creates a great musical comedy, but in real life making your way up to the top is not so easy. If you want to rise in positions at work, and stay there, you need to be able to do your job. For most people, doing a job well is the first step to leadership in a future career.

Practicing Leadership Skills
In junior high and high school, you probably will

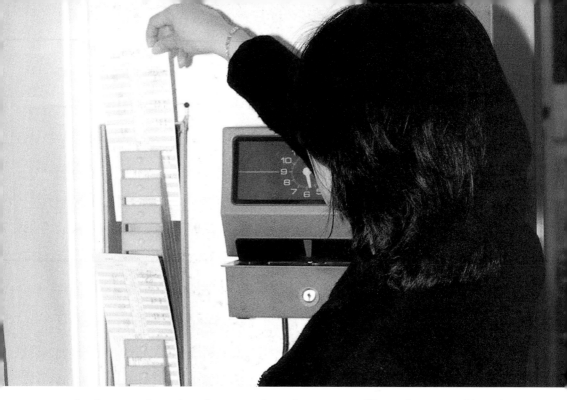

Coming to work on time shows your boss that you are willing to be responsible and work hard.

not get a job that puts you right into a leadership position. At this point in your life, you do not yet have the necessary experience or time to lead a company. In any work situation, however, you can still set yourself apart as a leader.

To do this, you first need to have positive work habits. Arrive at work on time all the time. Although you may not consider it a big deal, getting to work fifteen minutes late makes a difference to your employer. A prompt arrival sends a meaningful signal. It lets your boss know that you are reliable and ready to work. She or he can count on you to be there and get the job done.

Present yourself well by the way you look and act. The way you dress creates a significant impression. Although the clothing required to work in a fast-food restaurant, a toy store, or a business office varies, some common guidelines apply. Look at what the other employees are wearing, and dress similarly. This may require you to invest in some key wardrobe items, like dark pants, a white shirt, or a plain skirt, but a few well-chosen clothes combined in different ways can be all you need. Never look sloppy. Minor details, like wearing a belt, socks, or simple jewelry, do a lot to show that you care about the business's image. Try to look professional.

The way you communicate is important. Speak to everyone—customers, supervisors, and co-workers—with courtesy. The simple use of manners—saying please and thank you—may be what makes you stand out. When you are asked a question that requires a detailed answer, respond with more than, "Yes," "No," or "Uh-huh." Be honest and considerate. Listen carefully when you are given a task to complete. Ask questions if you need to, but once you know what you need to do, go to work.

Perhaps the most critical factor that can mark you as a leader is your attitude. Do you seem eager to do your job well? Try to avoid careless mistakes. Review the quality of your work before showing it to others. If you have extra time, ask your supervisor what else you can do, or search out projects yourself. Speak up if you want more responsibility. Look for ways to stay busy and productive.

Handling Conflict Creatively

Jonah works in the stockroom at Value Plus Supermarket. Over the past few months, he has gotten to know a few of the other high school kids who also have jobs there. One day after his shift is over, Jonah leaves work and forgets his jacket. When he goes back to get it, he notices Alex, another stock clerk, putting cans of soup into his gym bag. Alex does not see Jonah.

From then on, Jonah notices that Alex usually leaves work after everyone else. He also sees that Alex always brings a big gym bag. Jonah realizes that Alex probably steals from the supermarket all the time.

Jonah doesn't know what to do. He knows that stealing is wrong, and he remembers what the manager, Geoff, had said when he was hired.

"If I catch anyone taking anything, he's fired—and if I just see that food is missing, you're all fired!" Geoff had warned.

Jonah needs this job and is worried about Alex's stealing, but at the same time he doesn't want to report him and seem like a snitch. Jonah thinks about the situation and decides to say something casually when Alex is around.

"Hey Alex, did you ever notice that there are cans missing from some of these boxes? I wonder what's happening here?"

Alex shoots a glance at Jonah, then quickly looks back down at the box he is lifting.

"I don't know what you mean," he says curtly.

"Maybe I'm just paranoid because of what Geoff said my first day," says Jonah. "He made it sound like we're all fired if even one can is missing. I don't know about you, but I need this job."

Alex keeps looking down.

"Uh-huh," he mutters, trying to sound uninterested.

Alex has been stealing; now he realizes that Jonah knows what he is doing.

Jonah takes one more step to protect himself. He is worried that Alex might go to Geoff and say that he, Jonah, is the thief. So he decides to make a record of what has happened by telling his school counselor. Jonah makes an appointment to talk to the counselor and tells him the situation, knowing that everything he says will be kept confidential. This way, if Alex accuses Jonah of stealing, there is a trustworthy member of the community who can back up Jonah's story.

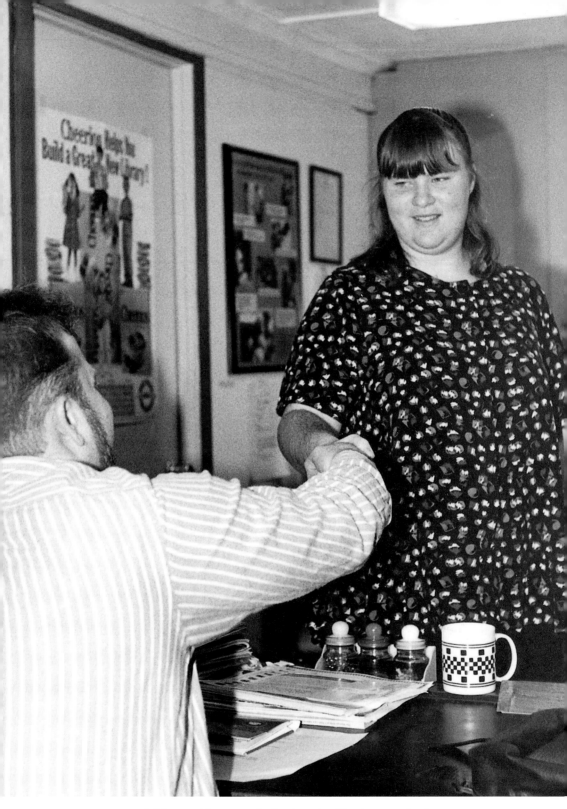

Solving problems creatively at work will get you noticed.

Jonah is smart to protect himself. He does not want to be blamed for something he hasn't done, and he is not sure how Alex will react. By making a record of what has happened with someone outside the workplace, Jonah takes steps to see that trying to solve this conflict does not backfire. Jonah just wants to keep his job and do it as best he can.

Jonah uses an important leadership skill by handling a conflict creatively. When he caught Alex stealing, Jonah had two obvious choices. One was to pretend he saw nothing, and the other was to report Alex to the manager. Neither possibility felt right to Jonah. So he created his own option. He brought up the issue of how missing food could affect the whole staff so that Alex would realize the full consequences of his actions. By doing this, Jonah warned Alex that he risked being caught, and he protected his own job without turning Alex in.

Being Visible

If you do your job well, the people who work with you will notice your commitment. This probably includes your manager, boss, or supervisor. A sensible manager will then do what is necessary to keep you around, whether that means a pay raise, a promotion, or simply steady employment. If your supervisor is not in the workplace often, be careful not to put on a show of hard work only when she or he shows up.

On weekends Raoul works as a waiter at Burger Bonanza, a local family restaurant. He makes a habit of arriving at the restaurant fifteen minutes before his shift begins. His red "Burger Bonanza" T-shirt is clean and unwrinkled. Even when the customers are rude, Raoul is polite no matter what. He always provides fast service.

Since the restaurant has outdoor seating, there are lots of customers when the weather is sunny. On days when it rains and business is slow, most of the other students who work there sit down at a table, get something to eat, and hang out. Raoul sometimes joins them, but only for a short while.

Usually, Raoul looks for ways to keep busy. He wipes tables and chairs, sweeps, refills condiment containers, and does all he can to keep the restaurant looking neat. Some of the other waiters start following Raoul's example. The manager, Terrance, notices Raoul's commitment to his job and talks to him one day after his shift his over.

"Hey, Raoul," Terrance begins, "you're a good worker."

"Thanks, I like it here," Raoul tells him.

"I can tell," Terrance says. "Listen, Raoul, remember when I hired you, I said I could only use

Make use of less busy hours at work to catch up on cleaning, stocking, and other tasks.

you for the spring? In a few weeks I've got all the college kids who worked here last summer coming back, and I told them they could have their old jobs. But I think that the way you work gets the rest of the kids going. I'd like you to stay on, if you want to."

"That would be great," Raoul says with a smile. He shakes Terrance's hand. "Thanks," he adds.

By using basic leadership techniques, Raoul has gotten himself a summer job when most of his friends can't find one. His hard work makes him a leader among the other waiters, who don't want to look lazy around him. Raoul's desire to work well is contagious.

Take the Initiative

No matter where you are working, you can take the initiative and start doing something that will improve the work you do. For example, if you are a baby-sitter, you might pick up the children's toys after they are asleep. If you are mowing lawns, you might also remove litter or rake leaves. If you deliver newspapers, be sure that they make it to the doorstep. Customers and employers appreciate good quality and service.

Any job offers you a learning opportunity. Even a bad work experience can teach you how *not* to run a business or how *not* to be a boss. If you are lucky, you may find work that helps you move toward your career. However, you can make the most of any work situation by trying out and developing your leadership skills.

Questions to Ask Yourself

There are many ways on the job to display positive work habits, responsibility, and motivation. 1) On the job, do you show positive work habits? 2) How do you handle conflicts with others? 3) Do you show your commitment to the job?

Moving Ahead in Your Career

HAVE YOU THOUGHT ABOUT WHAT YOU MIGHT choose as your life's work? Some students know from an early age what they would like to become eventually; others take many years to decide. Either way, you can use your talent, skills, and ability as a leader to help you explore different careers.

Getting an Education

A good education is a great asset. It gives you access to leadership positions that might be hard to reach otherwise. There are true stories of very successful people who did not go to school beyond the eighth grade, but they are rare. Usually people who don't graduate from high school find their career choices very limited.

A strong educational background looks impressive on a job application or résumé. It shows that you can learn, concentrate, and fulfill your goal by graduating. The more education you get, whether through high school, technical school, vocational training, college, or graduate school, the better off you will be.

In addition to your studies, you can get a valuable education outside the classroom. Organizations in your neighborhood, like your church, synagogue, community center, or fire department, can offer chances to become involved as a leader.

By volunteering at an agency or organization, you can learn about the work that the people there do. You can observe the leaders and notice how effective they are. Perhaps you can get an internship that would give you a role in an institution or company. By talking with people who have careers that appeal to you, you can find out about some of the most satisfying and most frustrating aspects of those occupations.

Ever since she was a little girl, Keesha has known that she wants to become a doctor. She finds the study of the human body fascinating. At school, Keesha takes all the science courses she can and studies extra hard in chemistry and biology. She also borrows books from the library on how the body works. She loves to read them, especially over the summer when she has more time.

One day Keesha wakes up with stomach pain. When it doesn't go away after a few days, Keesha goes to see her doctor, Dr. Gutstein. After describing her discomfort, Keesha adds, "I wonder if I have endometriosis?" Dr. Gutstein asks Keesha more about how she is feeling and makes a thorough exam. She decides that Keesha's condition is not as serious as endometriosis, but she lets Keesha know that she is impressed.

"Where did you learn about endometriosis, Keesha?" Dr. Gutstein asks.

"I read a lot," Keesha tells her, then adds a bit shyly, "I'd like to become a doctor too."

Dr. Gutstein is encouraging. "I think you'd be a great doctor, Keesha. You know, there's a program at Franklin General Hospital for young volunteers. You would help the hospital staff by delivering items to the patients, and it also gives you the chance to see how a hospital works from the inside."

"That sounds great," Keesha says excitedly. "How can I get in?"

"Here." Dr. Gutstein jots down a phone number on a piece of paper and hands it to her. "This is the hospital switchboard. Call and ask for the volunteer office. Ask about the junior volunteer program, and mention my name. I'd be glad to recommend you; I think you'd like it."

"Thanks, Dr. Gutstein," Keesha replies. She is eager to be part of the hospital community, so she can prepare herself for her career. And the experience will help her when she applies to college.

Asking for help from others who are more experienced is often necessary to achieve
your own goals.

Keesha's commitment to her studies and her eagerness to get some practical experience will move her toward her goal. If Keesha keeps her dream of becoming a doctor, she has an excellent chance of fulfilling it and becoming a leader in her community.

Having a Mentor

Keesha might also ask Dr. Gutstein to be her mentor. A mentor is someone who helps you advance from one point in your life to another. This person has experience and can teach you about a field or profession. Generally a mentor is someone whom you know personally and admire. Having a mentor is a great help as you move ahead in your career.

Some students may be part of a mentoring program set up by their school or the company where they work. If you are in this situation, you can make the most of it by meeting with your mentor regularly. Ask your mentor how she or he got to this position. What would she or he recommend that you do? What should you be careful not to do? Find out the key to your mentor's success, and see if it can open doors for you too.

If you are not part of a formal mentoring program, you can still find someone to be your mentor. A mentor might be a teacher, a clergyperson, or a relative. Is there someone whom you respect for what she or he has done? If so, tell the person, and ask for guidance. If there is no one you can think of to be your mentor, meet people through volunteering or ask your parents, teachers, or guidance counselor to help you find someone. Even the process of finding a mentor can help you develop your leadership skills.

Coaching Others

You might also act as a mentor yourself by coaching someone else. While coaching is usually associated with sports teams, it actually involves helping and encouraging others to reach any goal. If there is someone you know who needs help studying a subject or practicing for a competition in an area where you already have ability or experience, you can coach this person and practice leading one-on-one. You might also help coach a local soccer or Little League team, and closely observe the leadership style of the other coaches. Tell a teacher or counselor about your interest in gaining leadership skills. He or she will be able to advise you on programs like Big Brother/Big Sister or school tutoring programs. If your school does not have a tutoring program, perhaps you can be the person to start one.

Remember that praising people for what they do right usually encourages them to try hard to do it

Talk to parents, family friends, teachers, counselors, or other adults for advice on career planning.

well again. Coaches, tutors, and advisers who put others down end up discouraging them. Insulting players or participants results in less team spirit and drive to succeed. But praising what is being done right, and then instructing what can be done better, inspires the people you are coaching to move ahead.

Making Connections

As you move ahead in your work, get to know people in your career field. When you are looking for a job or seeking a better position, you increase your chances of getting it if you know someone who makes the hiring or promoting decisions.

If you are aware of this, you can make the right connections. If you have a mentor, you already have an important contact. Perhaps your mentor could introduce you to other influential people. If you don't know anyone yet who does what you would like to do, find a way to meet people in that field. You might volunteer with an agency that interests you. Perhaps there is an internship program that you could apply for. Find a way into a place that interests you personally and professionally.

Once you are there, show your capability and potential as a leader. Do your work well. When you appreciate a supervisor, let her or him know. Maybe even send a note saying what you have learned. If you move to another department or company, stay in touch. Having these connections might be very useful later in your career.

Questions to Ask Yourself

Sharpening your leadership skills now will pay off in your future job or career. 1) Have you given thought to what you want to do as a career? 2) How might you learn about a company or organization without having a job there? 3) Why is a mentor useful in getting ahead?

Lead On!

AS A LEADER, YOU HAVE A RESPONSIBILITY TO work with others toward a common goal. Because very few plans in life ever go perfectly, problems and conflicts will arise. Being a leader when all is going well can be easy. Handling difficult situations well is what makes a leader outstanding.

The first step to take when things go wrong is to face up to any mistakes you may have made. Suppose you've become editor-in-chief of the school newspaper. In an article welcoming the new principal, Dr. Caliendro, her name is misspelled. Deal with the situation head-on. Stop by her office before the article comes out and apologize. Write a correction piece for the next issue. Deal with the situation with grace and humor.

Another way to handle the blunder would be to get mad at the reporter who wrote the story or the proofreader who let the error slide by. But what good would that do? You would do far better not to make a scene and discourage or embarrass them. In

Be sure to review your work carefully to avoid careless mistakes.

private, you might gently ask them to double-check all names the next time. People appreciate it when you do not give up on them after one error.

When conflicts arise, confront them in a pro-active way. Bring the people who are involved together to talk about what is bothering them. Then they can get back to focusing on why they are working together in the first place, instead of on what is driving them apart.

Suppose you are the student director for the musical *Grease*. During rehearsal, Jodi, who plays Rizzo, mutters under her breath to her friends that Leslie, who plays Sandra Dee, sings flat. Her friends laugh, and Leslie figures out that they are making fun of her. Within two days, everyone in the show has taken either Jodi's or Leslie's side. When it comes time to stage the final number "We Go Together," the cast is very unconvincing.

You call a meeting to talk about everyone's problems. Leslie confronts Jodi, who apologizes. While some feelings are still bruised, at least people do not feel so divided. You remind the cast that the goal is to put on a good show, and problems shouldn't get in the way.

As a leader you need to keep perspective on what you are doing. Suppose you are the captain of the varsity basketball team. You are in great shape, and you're ready to bring the team into first place. But, despite your high expectations, your team has a so-so season. Last year four of your best players graduated, and the new team just hasn't had enough time together yet. But you feel that you let the team down.

Instead of getting depressed, try to look at the bigger picture. Remember that with your family, friends, and classes, everything is going fine. Remind yourself that the team's failure wasn't all your fault. Know that you tried hard, and take satisfaction from that knowledge.

Remember that being a leader is not like being a magician. It does not require an ability to make a dazzling and perfect presentation. Instead it involves community, effort, teamwork, and vision. If you can empower and inspire people to work with you toward meaningful goals, you are the kind of leader today's world needs.

Questions to Ask Yourself

Part of being a leader is dealing with situations when things go wrong. 1) Can you face up to mistakes you may make? 2) Are you able to take losing without being upset? 3) Can you keep a leader's perspective on your team's performance?

Glossary

accomplish To achieve, complete, or reach a goal.

ambition Drive to succeed.

capability Skill, know-how, potential.

commitment Dedication, follow-through.

crusader One who advances with zeal for a given cause.

delegate To assign tasks and responsibilities.

discriminate To prejudge unfairly based on features other than ability.

initiative The drive to start up or begin something; spirit, spunk.

leader One who is able to influence others, work together, and get things done.

motivate To get people excited about something and inspire them to take action.

priority Rank, list, or understanding of what is most important.

privilege An honor; an opportunity.

proactive Performing an action while being prepared for future problems, needs, or changes that may result.

reliable Believable, dependable.

For Further Reading

Blohowiak, Donald W. *Mavericks! How to Lead Your Staff to Think Like Einstein, Create Like DaVinci, and Invent Like Edison*. Homewood, IL: Business One Irwin, 1992.

Heifetz, Ronald A. *Leadership Without Easy Answers*. Cambridge, MA: Belknap Press, 1994.

Karnes, Frances A., and Bean, Suzanne M. *Girls and Young Women Leading the Way: 20 True Stories About Leadership*. Minneapolis: Free Spirit, 1993.

Levine, Stuart R., and Crom, Michael A. *The Leader in You: How to Win Friends, Influence People, and Succeed in a Changing World*. New York: Simon & Schuster, 1993.

Wills, Garry. *Certain Trumpets: The Call of Leaders*. New York: Simon & Schuster, 1994.

Index

About the Author

Julie Parker is an ordained minister in the United Methodist Church. She has written numerous books for teenagers.

Photos

Cover by Katherine Hsu; all other photos by Matthew Baumann and Kim Sonsky.

Layout and Design

Kim Sonsky